AUGUST

ESTES PARK, CO.

≡ A Portrait of ≡

ROCKY MOUNTAIN
NATIONAL PARK

by Jim Osterberg & James Frank

A Portrait of
Rocky Mountain
National Park
by Jim Osterberg & James Frank

Cataloging in Publication Data
Osterberg, Jim.
A Portrait of Rocky Mountain National Park
trade paperback ISBN 1-55265-032-4
hardcover ISBN 1-55265-033-2
1. Rocky Mountain National Park (Colo.)—Pictorial
works. I.
Frank, James. II. Title.
F782.R59087 1998   917.88'69   C98-910088-X

Production

Art direction/design	Stephen Hutchings
Design/layout	Kelly Stauffer
Editor	Sabrina Grobler
Financial manager	Laurie Smith

Printed in Canada by Friesen Printers
The photographs in this book have not been
digitally enhanced.

Altitude Green Tree Program
Altitude will plant in the United States twice as
many trees as were used in the manufacturing of
this product. This innovative program was created
and developed by Altitude Publishing in 1995.

Front cover
The vertical cliffs of Hallett Peak tower above
Dream Lake

title page
A mountain sunrise viewed from Rainbow Curve

back cover
top: A fall morning on the Mummy Range,
Hidden Valley
bottom: Coyote pups near the den

page 1
The image of Longs Peak is mirrored in this view
from the Bear Lake Nature Trail.

page 2-3
Dawn's early light casts a pink hue on Mt. Meeker
(left), Longs Peak (center) and Mt. Lady Washington
(right) in this view from Highway 7.

Contents

ROCKY MOUNTAIN NATIONAL PARK

Top: Glacier Creek tumbles down Glacier Gorge below Black Lake.

Opposite: Winter descends on the summit of Longs Peak while fall color is at its best in this Moraine Park aspen grove.

Rocky Mountain National Park contains 415 square miles of the most spectacular mountain scenery in America. With its granite summits towering over broad, forested valleys the landscape inspires the visitor with its immense size and beauty. To view this scene is to look back over 2 billion years. The mountaintops we see today contain metamorphic rocks created from remnants of a previous mountain range. Todays Rockies, formed by an uplift that began about 70 million years ago, are still changing. Only 16,000 to 22,000 years ago, glaciers were slowly shaping the steep mountain faces that form Rocky's stunning scenery. The erosive forces of ice and the rocks trapped within it sculpted out

7

Top Early morning light illuminates the Mummy Range above the meandering Fall River in Horseshoe Park.

Bottom: Referred to locally as "Fan Lake," this body of water was created on July 15, 1982 by an unexpected breach of the Lawn Lake dam. The resulting, sudden release of 674 acre feet of water and the debris carried with it dammed the Fall River, creating the lake. It is now slowly draining away.

Top: Golden banner blooms in June along the Big Thompson River in Moraine Park. The mountains of the Mummy Range are on the horizon.

broad U-shaped valleys from old river channels, adding drama to the view. Slowly the ice receded, depositing debris to form giant ridges of rock rubble. Called moraines, these ridges trapped water from the melting ice, creating lakes that eventually filled with sediments to become lush meadows. Even today, five glaciers remain on some north-facing slopes and, bit by bit, rivers continue to carry away eroded materials from the mountains.

In 1909, Enos Mills, who led the campaign to form a national park in the Estes Park area, described the resources that warranted the establishment of Rocky Mountain National Park:

> *Around Estes Park, Colorado, are mountain scenes of such beauty and grandeur. In this territory is Longs Peak and one of the most rugged sections of the Continental Divide of the Rockies. The region is almost entirely above the altitude of 7,500 feet, and in it are forests, streams, waterfalls, snowy peaks, great canyons, glaciers, scores of species of wild birds, and more than athousand varieties of wildflowers.*

Top: Golden early morning light and the opportune arrival of a kingfisher combine in this unusual photo of Sprague Lake.

Opposite: Snowcapped peaks along the Continental Divide are reflected in the calm waters of Sprague Lake in Glacier Basin.

Following: Tyndall Creek passes boulders and bedrock below Emerald Lake. The craggy spires of Flattop Mountain touch the sky above.

His efforts were successful and this wild treasure was officially recognized on January 26, 1915, when it became our tenth national Park. Soon, it came under the protection of the newly formed National Park Service with its mandate to "...conserve the scenery and the natural and historic objects and the wildlife therein and to provide for the enjoyment of the same in such manner and by such means as will leave them unimpaired for the enjoyment of future generations."

A major challenge indeed! One that requires our cooperation as Park visitors as well as constant work, diligence and great wisdom on the part of Park management professionals.

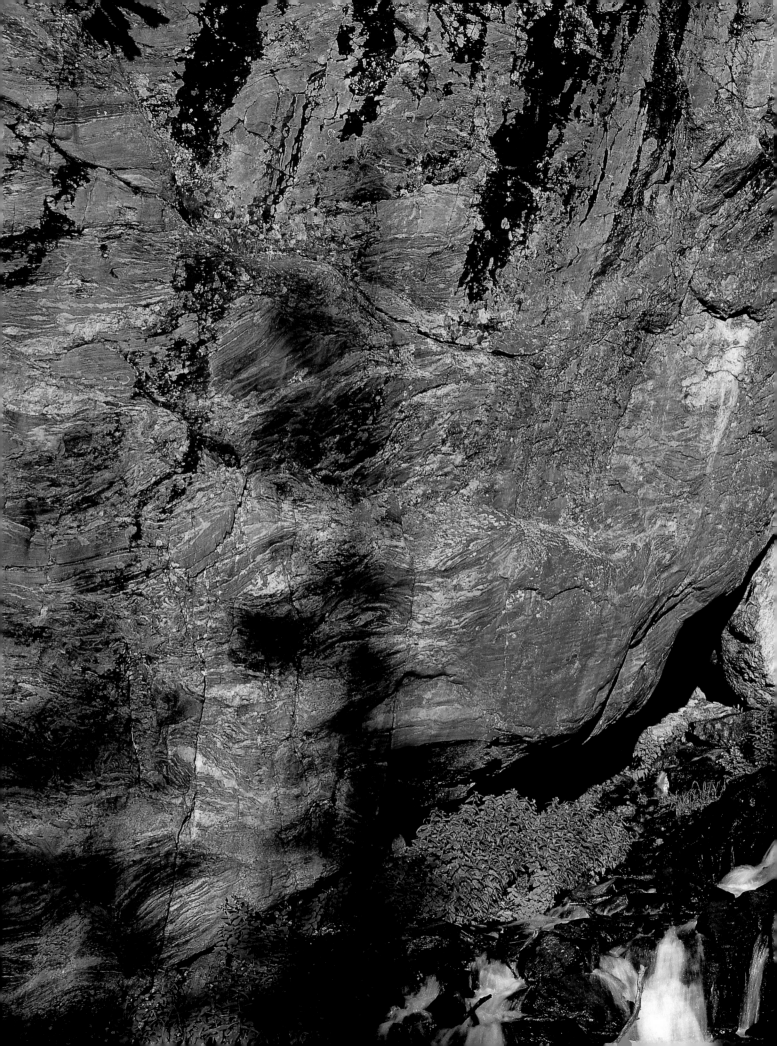

ESTES PARK

Top: The town of Estes Park, viewed from the summit of Mt. Olympus.

Opposite: Riverside Plaza along the Fall River in downtown Estes Park comes alive with summer flowers.

At an elevation of roughly 7,500 feet, the community of Estes Park occupies one of the most beautiful valleys in the American West. Imagine the view in 1859 when Joel Estes and his son, Milton, wandered into this glorious valley. The area now occupied by Lake Estes was an open meadow, endowed with the meandering Big Thompson River. This environment offered sustenance to herds of elk, deer and bighorn sheep. In adjacent forests, grizzly and black bears foraged berries and roots. At night, the calls of wolves and coyotes split the starry skies. Small wonder that the Earl of Dunraven attempted a dozen years later to make the Estes Valley his private hunting preserve. It is fortunate for all he did not succeed.

Natural beauty wasn't the only reason people came to the Estes Valley. Native Americans found the hunting good and were able to access points west through several routes over the mountains. Prospectors came seeking riches from the earth. Homesteaders like Joel Estes and Griff Evans hunted and tried their luck

Top: Longs Peak dominates the skyline in this panoramic scene of the Front Range, viewed from The Needles on Lumpy Ridge.

Left: Winter snow dusts the Twin Owls formation on Lumpy Ridge in late afternoon.

at raising cattle. Adventurers and visitors came seeking the challenge of high peaks and the beauty of the land. The feeding, lodging and guiding of these visitors became the essential commerce of the area.

At the turn of the century, the future of Estes Park was being shaped by people like F.O. Stanley, who with his brother invented the Stanley Steamer automobile. He visited Estes Park in 1903, and within several years, he and a partner purchased the 6,400 acre Dunraven estate. In 1909 he opened the luxurious Stanley Hotel, attracting wealthy visitors and helping to make Estes Park one of America's premier vacation destinations. Through the efforts of men like F.O. Stanley, Enos Mills, and Abner Sprague, a trend of growth with an eye to the tourist had begun. The town's destiny was set. Today, Estes Park continues to host travelers from all over the world.

At the heart of Estes Park, two rivers come together to form a confluence which the town has honored by building a beautiful downtown Park called Riverside Plaza. A system of paved trails following the Big Thompson and Fall Rivers connects Riverside Plaza with a series of smaller town Parks. These rivers begin high in snowfields nestled among mountain peaks to the west. River sources and mountains are forever protected in the neighboring Rocky Mountain National Park.

Top: Wildflowers brighten this view of Estes Valley from Highway 7.

Bottom: These wapiti or American elk spend a leisurely spring day in Estes Park.

Top left: A section of the Riverwalk follows the Big Thompson River through Estes Park.

Top right: One of many wildlife sculptures located in Estes Park, this life-sized eagle soars in perpetual flight over Riverside Plaza.

Bottom: Rocky Mountain National Park Headquarters and Beaver Meadows Visitor Center is located on U.S. Highway 36 at the entrance to the Park.

PEAK-TO-PEAK & LONGS PEAK

Top: The Lily Lake Visitor Center welcomes travelers on Highway 7.

Opposite: Mt. Meeker, elevation 13,911 feet, stands guard along the Peak to Peak Scenic and Historic Byway.

Known locally as the Peak to Peak Highway, the Peak to Peak Scenic and Historic Byway was established in 1918 and is Colorado's oldest scenic byway. Fifty-five miles in length, it runs south from Estes Park on Colorado Highway 7, through the scenic Tahosa Valley, past Allenspark all the way to the towns of Central City and Blackhawk. Although no part of the Peak to Peak is inside Rocky Mountain National Park, it roughly parallels the Park's eastern boundary and offers magnificent views of the Park's highest mountains.

"Scenic and historic" is a well-deserved designation. The Byway passes

numerous historic sites including the Baldpate Inn, Enos Mills' Cabin and Meeker Park Lodge. It's no wonder that early settlers like Elkanah Lamb and Enos Mills chose the scenic Tahosa Valley south of Lily Lake and Wind River Pass for their homesteads. It was from this valley that Enos Mills guided many visitors to the summit of Longs Peak and inspired many more with writings and lectures of his experiences in this rugged paradise.

The popular drive on the Peak to Peak Byway between Estes Park and Wild Basin near Allenspark is remarkable for its geological and natural history as well as for its breathtaking scenery. Glaciation is evident in the valley of the Roaring Fork stretching down from Longs Peak, and in the U-shaped valley of the North St. Vrain Creek. At the entrance to Wild Basin, near Copeland Lake, the North St. Vrain is surrounded by a willow wetland-great habitat for numerous bird species. Named "Wild Basin" by Enos Mills, the area to the west is one of the most remote and wild in the Park.

Longs Peak, flanked by Mt. Meeker and Mt. Lady Washington, dominates the western skyline along this section of the Byway. This massive rock, composed of Precambrian granite, is a study of earth history. Over eons, the powerful natural forces of uplift and erosion shaped and reshaped the face of the land.

Top: The Mummy Range looms over Estes Valley in this early morning view from Highway 7 near Lily Lake.

Bottom: Another clear summer morning dawns at Lily Lake.

The creative pulse of nature is revealed starkly in the Diamond, where Ice Age glaciers sculpted the sheer wall of the East Face. In the early morning light, the Diamond is at its most dramatic.

Longs Peak inspires all those who view it. Historic Arapaho and Ute Indians used Longs and the neighboring Mt. Meeker to orient their travels, calling the pair the Two Guides. Viewed from the semiarid high plains to the east, its form commands the Front Range skyline. Major Stephen H. Long and his Yellowstone Expedition first saw the Rocky Mountains on June 30, 1820. They were unified in their admiration of the distant mountains. Longs Peak, clearly the tallest of the range, was later named after this expeditionary leader.

Years later, adventurers like William Byers, a prominent editor of The Rocky Mountain News and an avid

Top: Colorful fall aspen couple with brilliant blue skies to frame this portrait of Mt. Meeker (left), Longs Peak (center) and Mt. Lady Washington (right) over the Tahosa Valley.

Opposite top: The Diamond on the East Face of Longs Peak glows at sunrise above Chasm Lake.

Opposite bottom: Ouzel Creek cascades over solid rock on its way to joining North St. Vrain Creek in Wild Basin.

mountaineer, were compelled to achieve the Longs Peak summit. On his second attempt in 1868, Byers accompanied explorer John Wesley Powell and his Colorado Scientific Exploring Expedition on a successful climb. This climb was the first known summit ascent. More importantly, Byers wrote about his experience, bringing wide acclaim to the mountain, the challenges it offered and the stunning natural beauty of the region.

Longs Peak remains a catalyst for thought and adventure. Thousands of hikers and climbers attempt to reach its summit every year. Not all succeed, but those who try experience a unifying sense of spirit and hard reality-a momentary harmonizing of the intuitive and rational minds. Some of the rewards are felt immediately. Others require a calming of the senses and distant reflection. Experience on the mountain often leads to a better understanding of self and the place one occupies in the natural world. Take nothing for granted. Keep an open mind. As Longs Peak climber Isabella Bird, the second woman to reach the summit, reflected, "In one's imagination it grows to be much more than a mountain."

Opposite: Columbine Falls. The Diamond, a vertical cliff dominating the east face of Longs Peak, is in the background.

Top left: Sunrise casts a glow on this Beaver Meadows aspen grove.

Top right: Stars and stripes catch a winter breeze beneath Longs Peak.

Bottom: The Beaver formation ascends the Diamond on the East Face of Longs Peak.

NATURE

Top: Bighorn sheep entertain visitors at Forest Canyon Overlook.

Bottom: During the fall "rut," sounds of bugling elk echo across mountain meadows.

Opposite: Bighorn ram

Overleaf left Cow elk enjoy a colorful snack of quaking aspen.

Overleaf right: Bull elk gather in a spring meadow near MacGregor Ranch.

29

Top: Bull moose in velvet

Left: Mountain lion, common but seldom seen

Right: Mule deer (doe)

Above: Coyote pups by den

Top left: Least chipmunk

Top right: Golden-mantled ground squirrel

Bottom left: Pika

Bottom middle: Yellow-bellied marmot

Bottom right: Chickaree

Top right: Great horned owl
Bottom right: White-tailed ptarmigan
Top left: Great Horned owlets in nest
Middle left: American robins
Bottom left: Steller's jay

Top left: Bald eagle

Bottom left: Golden eagle

Top right: Clark's nutcracker

Middle right: Grey jay

Bottom right: Magpie

Aspen grove

Alpine sunflowers (rydbergia) and tufted phlox

Black-eyed Susan

Indian paintbrush

Ponderosa pine, spring growth

Rocky Mountain iris

Above: Strong, almost constant winds at timberline shape these trees into a form often referred to as "banner trees."

Top right: Calypso orchid

Top left: Pasqueflower

Bottom right: Colorado blue columbine, state flower

Bottom left: Parry's primrose

Moraine Park

Top: Moraine Park Museum is a center for learning about Rocky's past and present.

Opposite: Autumn foliage brightens this view along the Big Thompson River in Moraine Park.

Moraine Park provides a richly threaded tapestry of human, geologic and natural history to all who take time to visit and observe. In dramatic fashion, this peaceful valley can guide us on a journey of discovery in a place where wilderness and humanity meet.

Like the early settlers, who came to Moraine Park in the mid 1870s, modern-day visitors marvel at its scenic and natural wonders. In 1875, Abner Sprague and his family were the first pioneers to homestead in the meadows then known as Willow Park, laying claim to 165 acres. Much like their neighbors in Estes Park, Sprague and those who followed soon found out that catering to visitors provided a much better living than raising cattle. Winters were tough, but over time private resort cabins and lodges were built as the hospitality trade flourished and the Moraine Park community grew, complete with its

39

own 9 hole golf course.

Some cabins can still be seen today as "grandfathered" inholdings, offering a mere glimpse of this past development.

Today's Moraine Park Museum, built in 1923 and purchased by the Park Service in 1936, originally served as a social gathering place, dance hall and tea-room for residents and travelers. Through its numerous exhibits, tapes, films and books, the museum is an educational resource center for learning about Moraine Park and Rocky Mountain National Park. It is listed on the National Register of Historic Places.

A walk on the interpretive trail near the Moraine Park Museum offers fresh mountain air, facts about plants and animals, and an uncommon view of a living landscape that nature has made and remade over the milennia.

Bordering Moraine Park on the north and south are long forested ridges called glacial moraines. On the right is the north lateral moraine, where ponderosa pine forests grow on drier, south-facing slopes. On the left is the south lateral moraine. On these slopes with greater shade, where soils hold more moisture, lodgepole and ponderosa pine mix with Douglas fir. The Big Thompson River meanders through the valley floor, creating prime wetland habitat.

Top: This panoramic view shows the diversity of ecosystems seen from the Moraine Park Museum. The Big Thompson River meanders across the valley floor below montane and subalpine forests reaching to the peaks of the Continental Divide.

Right: Morning fog shrouds the valley floor around a glacial feature called a Roche moutonnée (French for "sheep rock"). This bedrock knob withstood the erosive actions of glaciers.

Overleaf: Spruce Canyon, viewed from Moraine Park.

BEAR LAKE

Top: Soft light and an unusually quiet morning combine to make a perfect reflection of Longs Peak in Bear Lake.

Opposite: A bright blue summer morning sky reflects in the Big Thompson River at Moraine Park.

In the idyllic setting of Bear Lake, one feels close to the mountains. Couched in a rocky basin, the lake is surrounded by dense forests of spruce, fir and pine. Above, the glacially sculpted peaks command the view and illustrate a geological heritage of ice and snow. Long ago, the Bartholf Glacier and its tributaries filled the cirque basins and valleys. After countless freeze-thaw cycles, loosened rock fragments were quarried from mountainsides by glacial action. The glaciers then carried the rocks along as grinding stones, thereby widening the V-shaped river valleys, steepening the mountainsides and creating the distinctive U-shaped valleys we see today. Examples of this quarrying action can be seen from the parking lot in the sheer, vertical cliffs on Hallett Peak and Flattop Mountain.

At an elevation of 9,475 feet, Bear Lake is the only subalpine lake in Rocky

Top: Every few years, when conditions are right, the aspen turn bright orange and red as in this grove along Bear Lake Road.

Bottom: Snowcapped mountains and golden aspen color this autumn scene above Bear Lake.

Top: Bear Lake Road winds through a forest of conifer and aspen below the towering presence of Longs Peak.

Mountain National Park that can be reached by car, making it one of the most popular and most visited areas in the park. The 0.6 mile nature trail around the lake is a casual stroll that rewards the nature lover with an educational and visually rewarding experience. The ranger station offers a variety of reading material about the area, including an informative nature booklet. The Bear Lake Trail is paved and wheelchair accessible.

The names of prominent features in the region gesture toward early historic accounts. Bear Lake was named by Horace Ferguson who, while hunting deer and elk near the lake, spotted and shot at a bear with his old muzzle-loading rifle. Ferguson lived to tell the tale and name the lake. Arapaho Indians called the sharp-edged peak cutting the sky above Bear Lake "Thunder Cloud Peak," an appropriate name given the frequent storms that cloak its summit. Known today as Hallett Peak, the mountain was named in 1887 by Frederick Chapin, an avid mountaineer who was competently guided above Bear Lake by William Hallett.

In 1900 a fire, known as the Bear Lake Fire or Big Fire, began near Bear Lake as a picnic campfire that was not completely doused. Fanned by winds, the blaze raged for two months and burned vast areas of forest. The fire burned so

Top: Fall arrives in Glacier Basin in this view of Hallett Peak (left) and Flattop Mountain (right) from Bear Lake Road. Tyndall Glacier is visible in the gorge between the mountains.

Left: Quaking aspen in the spring frame this scene of Bear Lake with Longs Peak, Pagoda Mountain and Chiefs Head on the skyline.

Right: Winter snow blankets Glacier Creek.

Following page: Morning calm offers peaceful reflections of Hallett Peak and subalpine forest in Bear Lake.

hot in some areas that it cracked granite boulders. Photographs taken after the fire show charred, near-barren slopes. Nearly a century later, little evidence of the fire remains, a strong testament of nature's ability to reclaim the land.

Like spokes on a wheel with Bear Lake at its hub, hiking trails fan out into wild and steep glacial cirques with lakes that glisten like watery pearls, connected by shimmering strands of clear mountain streams. A hike into the gorge between Hallett and Flattop should not be missed. The Emerald Lake Trail starts at Bear Lake and connects a series of lakes named Bear, Nymph, Dream and Emerald. A short but sometimes steep trail ascends step-like bedrock cliffs that resisted glacial erosion.

Each of the lakes affords a completely different, yet equally striking view of Hallett Peak. Yellow pondlilies dot Nymph Lake in the summer; the clear waters of Tyndall

Top: Otis and Hallett peaks touch the azure sky above this grove of brilliant quaking aspen.

Left: One of several small cirque lakes in the Bear Lake area, Nymph Lake is a short half- mile walk from Bear Lake.

Creek pass beneath bridges on the approach to Dream Lake; rocky outcrops on the shore of Dream Lake are great places to stop for lunch and enjoy the view of Hallett. On these outcrops grow limber pine so exquisitely shaped by the elements and prevailing westerly winds that they might have materialized from a dream. Above the lake, a cutoff trail leads to Lake Haiyaha in Chaos Canyon. The main trail to Emerald Lake follows Tyndall Creek, originating at Tyndall Glacier high in the saddle between the two mountains. Tyndall Glacier is one of several glaciers still remaining in the park. Emerald Lake sparkles at the base of cliffs on Hallett and Flattop and is exactly what its name describes-one of Rocky's most easily reached high-elevation jewels.

Additional hikes from Bear Lake reach Glacier Gorge Junction, leading to exhilarating backcountry treks into Glacier Gorge and Loch Vale and passing Alberta Falls on the way. At the northeast corner of Bear Lake, steep trails lead to the Continental Divide over Flattop Mountain and to Odessa Gorge below Notchtop and Knobtop Mountains. A less strenuous hike amidst verdant forest cuts east from the same trailhead to Bierstadt Lake, atop a moraine that bears the same name. While you are in the Bear Lake basin, be sure to allow yourself enough time to enjoy the outstanding examples of nature's handiwork.

Opposite: Dream Lake is a pleasant 1.1 mile hike above Bear Lake.

Top left: Snow-fed Glacier Creek cascades through Glacier Gorge.

Top right: Morning sun warms The Loch near the eastern portal of Loch Vale.

Bottom right: Mills Lake in Glacier Gorge is a popular hiking destination.

OLD FALL RIVER ROAD & TRAIL RIDGE ROAD

Top: Vibrant sunset hues add color to this view of Longs Peak from Rock Cut on Trail Ridge.

Opposite: Beavers constantly build dams to create the ponds in which they live. As these ponds fill with silt, the beavers will move to a new stream location.

For many, the trip over the "roof of the Rockies" is the highlight of a visit to Rocky Mountain National Park. With a choice of routes—Old Fall River Road or Trail Ridge Road—grand vistas reward the traveler. The relatively short, 48 mile trip from Estes Park to Grand Lake climbs from just under 8,000 feet to over 12,000 feet and traverses through three distinct ecosystems.

Starting on the east side at an elevation of 7,800 feet, the road winds through an open, relatively dry montane forest of ponderosa pine and small aspen groves. Large meadows, called "parks" by early pioneers, separate the forest.

Remnants of glacial lakes long ago filled by sediments, the rich soils of these meadows produce lush grasses that sustain herds of elk. On the edges, where the meadow meets the forest, mule deer and other wildlife find perfect conditions in which to thrive.

At about 9,000 feet, a dense forest of subalpine fir and Engelmann spruce covers the slopes and stands of lodgepole pine, a tall, slender tree favored by the Ute Indians for teepee poles, reclaim areas where the forest has burned. This is the subalpine ecosystem, home to birds, squirrels, snowshoe hare, bobcats and a few migrating deer or elk.

Eventually, at an elevation of 11,000 to 11,500 feet, the trees begin to lose their struggle against the harsh alpine conditions and with the exception of a few windblown subalpine fir and Engelmann spruce and an occasional gnarled, twisted limber pine, the trees surrender to a near-arctic environment. This is the alpine ecosystem, a fragile world of tundra where stunted vegetation grows close to the ground. Trees, if they manage to take root here, grow as krummholz on the lee side of rocks or in gullies, where they are protected from the driving wind.

Top: Rays of sunlight over Horseshoe Park promise an end to one of the frequent afternoon thunderstorms that occur during early summer.

Previous top: This summer view of the Mummy Range and Horseshoe Park shows the alluvial fan, visible near the center of the photo.

Previous bottom: Winter's mantle crowns peaks in the Mummy Range in this vista above Horseshoe Park.

Top left: Chasm Falls is a favorite stop along Old Fall River Road.

Top right: Wildflowers grace the banks of the Fall River's upper reaches.

Bottom: Old Fall River Road winds through subalpine forest near tree line below the west slope of Mt. Chapin.

Left: The character of Horseshoe Falls was changed dramatically by the Lawn Lake Flood in 1982. Tumultuous waters, packing incredible force, carried boulders of all sizes that scoured the Roaring River drainage. When the floodwaters hit the valley floor, they slowed and spread, dropping rock debris as an alluvial fan.

Top: Fall aspen and forested slopes near Endovalley reflect in Fan Lake below Fall River Canyon.

At this elevation the growing season is short, so plants must make the best of the time they have. In early summer the tundra can explode in a symphony of color as a myriad of flowers bloom. It is important to enjoy the show from the highway or developed trails as walking on tundra plants can cause damage that will take hundreds of years to restore. This is the home of bighorn sheep, elk (in summer), marmot and pika.

At Milner Pass, Trail Ridge Road crosses the Continental Divide, the watershed point at which rivers flow east to the Atlantic or west to the Pacific oceans. West of the divide, precipitation is almost twice that on the east, promoting dense forest growth that extends to the valley floors. It is on this side that the Colorado River is born, gathering water from snowmelt as it begins its flow through the Kawuneeche Valley to empty eventually into the Pacific Ocean. Dominating the horizon, the Never Summer Range forms the Park's western boundary. Just ahead are Grand Lake, Colorado's largest natural lake, and the village of Grand Lake, the western gateway to Rocky Mountain National Park.

Top: Timberline trees like this limber pine are shaped by persistent, westerly winds into patterns of unusual rhythm and beauty.

Bottom: Fall storms sometimes fill Hidden Valley with low clouds, accenting distinctive aspen groves on the ridge above.

Opposite: Mts. Chapin (left), Chiquita (center) and Ypsilon (right) reflect in this fall view of the Hidden Valley Beaver Ponds.

Left: Coyotes can be found throughout the park as they search for food in all habitats from valley floors to the tundra.

Top: The rolling alpine landscape at Tundra Curves represents terrain that lay beyond the reach of glaciers.

Previous pages:
Left: Longs Peak towers over Forest Canyon in this view from Rock Cut on Trail Ridge Road.
Right: This July landscape on Trail Ridge is adorned with rydbergia, commonly called alpine sunflowers. Gorge Lake's cirque below Mt. Ida is seen across Forest Canyon.

Top: A precipitous view from Rock Cut shows Terra Tomah and Mt. Julian on the horizon.

Bottom: Through courageous efforts by Park Service personnel, Trail Ridge Road is cleared of snow each spring, affording unique views from above the trees.

Overleaf: The massif of Longs Peak, the Rockies' northernmost "14er," stands above the autumn tundra on Trail Ridge.

Top: The Alpine Visitor Center and Trail Ridge Store on Fall River Pass catch the final rays of the sun as it sets over the Never Summer Mountains.

Bottom: Located just east of the Continental Divide at Milner Pass, Poudre Lake is the headwaters of the Cache la Poudre River.

Bottom: Alpine avens bloom on the tundra near the Alpine Visitors Center. Trail Ridge Road and the Never Summer Mountains are in the background.

GRAND LAKE

Top: Sailing is a popular pastime on Grand Lake.

Opposite: Adams Falls is located on a small stream that flows into Grand Lake from the east. The falls are a short 0.3 mile hike from the East Inlet trailhead near Grand Lake.

The Kawuneeche Valley, named from the Arapaho term meaning "valley of the coyote," is one of the largest glacial valleys in the Park and serves as the drainage route for the Colorado River. Originating high in the mountains as a collection of small springs and rivulets fed by melting snow, the Colorado River rapidly gathers strength to become the nation's sixth longest river; it flows 1,400 miles to drain into the Pacific Ocean at the Gulf of California. Along the way it accomplishes such feats as carving the Grand Canyon and providing water and power to much of the western United States.

For years the river has attracted the attention of developers and agricultural interests seeking to acquire its water. One of the first projects of this kind was the construction of the Grand Ditch. Building this 14.3 mile canal began in 1890 and was completed in 1936. Water is diverted through the ditch into the Poudre River drainage for use on the drier east-side plains of the Front Range. The Grand Ditch is visible on the mountainsides across the valley.

Top: Morning sun reflects in Lake Granby with the mountains of Indian Peaks Wilderness in the distance.

Bottom: Beaver ponds help create wetland habitat in the Kawuneeche Valley. The Grand Ditch is visible in the top left.

Opposite top: Shadow Mountain Reservoir is the first of several impoundments on the Colorado River.

Opposite bottom: Never Summer Mountains command the western skyline above the Colorado River.

Long before it was discovered by early explorers, this area was a center of human activity. Generations of Indians hunted elk and deer and harvested other foods in and around the valley. Later, miners hoping to find gold or silver arrived. Their efforts proved futile, as did attempts to homestead in the area. Soon its real value became apparent. Dude ranches that catered to visitors who wanted a "western experience" were formed and the new industry was off and running. One of the first was the Never Summer Ranch which began operation in 1917 and prospered after the opening of Fall River Road in 1920. The ranch, no longer in operation, is preserved as an historic site and is open to park visitors.

The village of Grand Lake with its rich frontier-town history has been a destination and supply point for visitors to the area for over 100 years. Today, it is the western gateway to Rocky Mountain National Park.

W e hope this book will rekindle fond memories of your visit to Rocky Mountain National Park and inspire a sense of stewardship toward the land and wildlife portrayed on these pages. As you experience this beautiful, dynamic landscape, seize the opportunity to discover and learn more about the natural history of the Park and our relationship with this natural wonder. Armed with knowledge, we can better appreciate the Park's value as a national treasure and legacy to be preserved for future generations. The more we understand and respect our natural world, the more we will be able to experience and enjoy the wonder and

ABOUT THE AUTHORS

Jim Osterberg

For Jim Osterberg, who has served for several years as an interpreter for the V.I.P. Rocky Mountain National Park program, photography is both a profession and a lifestyle. Having lived in Colorado since 1973, he has spent 25 years photographing the wildlife and natural splendors of parks and preserves in the western United States. He has won numerous awards for his audiovisual work and his photographs have been featured in books and many publications such as *American Park Network*, *Colorado Outdoors*, *Country America*, *Geo* and the *Estes Park Watchable Wildlife Guide*, which he also wrote and produced. Jim operates a stock photography and brochure production business in Estes Park.

Osterberg's leisure pursuits are an integral part of his career; he takes advantage of his camping, hiking, snowshoeing and skiing excursions to document the beauty of his surroundings. He lives in Estes Park, Colorado with his wife and has two daughters.

James Frank

A longtime musician and professional photographer, James Frank seeks to represent in his photographs the rhythm and harmony of the natural world. He blends a long-standing love of the outdoors with his profession. His regard for the region's landscape resonates in his work, a fact that is evident to those who are inspired by it.

Frank is known for his exquisite limited-edition prints. One of his prints was chosen by the Superintendent of Rocky Mountain National Park as a gift to the Emperor Akihito and Empress Michiko of Japan in 1994. His work is widely published in books and magazines, as well as in advertising for clients including *Reader's Digest*, Bass Pro Shops and Texaco. Maintaining his stock and assignment photography business in Estes Park, James resides there with his wife and baby daughter.